Also by William Parkhurst

How to Get Publicity

THE
ELOQUENT
EXECUTIVE

THE
ELOQUENT
EXECUTIVE

A GUIDE TO
HIGH-IMPACT SPEAKING IN
BIG MEETINGS, SMALL MEETINGS,
AND ONE-ON-ONE

WILLIAM PARKHURST

𝕮imes BOOKS

Library of Congress Cataloging-in-Publication Data
Parkhurst, William.
    The eloquent executive.
    1. Business communication.   2. Oral communication.
3. Public speaking.   I. Title.
HF5718.P35   1988   658.4'52   87-40590
ISBN 0-8129-1280-2 (soft)

Designed by Robert Bull Design

Manufactured in the United States of America

9 8 7 6 5 4 3 2

First Edition

To Carolyn

ACKNOWLEDGMENTS

With special thanks to Robert Kimmel, Alan Steinberg, David Shanen, Dr. Emmanuel Zane, Geralyn Ross, Sandee Brawarsky, Marge Anderson, Bill Hughes, Mel Kaiser, Andrew Carlin, David Peretz, Peg Bailey, Susan Wernerts Lewis, Thomas Lashnits, Dennis Hermanson, Michael Schwager, my agent, Julian Bach, and especially my editor, Hugh O'Neill.

CONTENTS

THE
ELOQUENT
EXECUTIVE

1

INTRODUCTION

FOR MANY YEARS, clients and colleagues have asked me to recommend a speech book aimed at helping executives deliver their presentations in the tough, no-time-for-anything environment of modern corporate life. They wanted the essentials of high impact speaking without the extras. They agreed that theory, physiological diagrams, and thorough explanations of the speaking process were worthy of their attention, but right now, just the basics—what works and what doesn't—would be enough.

3

I couldn't find that book, so I wrote it. *The Eloquent Executive* is a speech program for management people who, under the heat of corporate demands, are expected to sound as good as they look when they present an idea. I first developed the program more than a decade ago when, as a publicity director for a publishing company, I began to train authors for their radio and television appearances. Producers demand that a guest be able to condense complex ideas into a few powerful sentences, and not lose his or her cool when questioned by such pros as Diane Sawyer, Mike Wallace, Barbara Walters, and Ted Koppel.

Five years ago, I expanded the plan to help executives prepare for sales conferences, trade shows, panels, seminars, and other everyday corporate situations. *The Eloquent Executive* goes beyond platform speaking to meeting presentations, one-to-one communication, business lunches, social occasions, and other corporate settings. It spells out what to do, when to do it, how to do it, and, sometimes, when to say nothing.

The Eloquent Executive is a program of strategies. I accept time as your most scarce, most valuable resource. Each chapter gives you a no-frills rundown on the best way to handle a speaking situation. Everything you need is right in front of you, and by the numbers. If you have less than a half hour to get a presentation written, it's all in Chapter 4, "The Fast Way to Write Your Talk." If you want to get psyched before you speak, Chapter 10, "Just Before You Speak," will show you how. Each chapter finishes with an Instant Review that can be gone over in seconds, if seconds is all you have.

4

We start with the basics, the ten high impact essentials that apply every time out, whether you're in a conference room or the Hollywood Bowl. Next comes an "Audience Analysis Checklist," "The Fast Way to Write Your Talk," and chapters that cut through the confusion to show you what goes in and stays out of the introduction, main body, and conclusion of your talk.

"High Impact Language" will help you compose a lean, muscular presentation free of those tired old clichés about challenges and the future.

Five chapters on delivery follow: "The Body Language of the Take-Charge Speaker," "Just Before You Speak," "Powervoicing," "The Q&A Session," and "Working with Visuals."

The book's final chapters, "Tips for Presenting at Meetings," "Defending Against Criticism Without Appearing Defensive," "Head to Head: Effective Presentations to a Single Individual," "The Business Lunch," "Cocktails at Seven, Dinner at Eight," and "The Eloquence of the Good Listener," give you the tools for a high impact performance in everyday work settings.

The Eloquent Executive is a primer. It's not supposed to tell you everything. If it inspires you to read more about speech, or take a course, I'll be thrilled, for I see speaking as a miracle. But if you come away with a little more awe for brevity, that will be enough. As George S. Kaufman said, "If I had time, I'd have written a shorter letter." I think I know what he would have said about today's business meetings and presentations.

2

BASIC
TRAINING

TEN BASICS apply to your talk whether you're arguing for better inventory control in a conference room or unveiling the new logo before a banquet audience of fifteen hundred.

1. Know Your Introduction and Conclusion Cold

If you can recite the beginning and end of a talk in your sleep, the middle will fall into place. Don't ever *memorize*, but knowing precisely where to start and stop assures that you'll launch your-self well and come in for a smooth landing. That's about all they're going to remember anyway.

2. Put the Details on a Handout Sheet

Most business speakers think they have to present enough minutiae to give everyone in the room, including the waiters and waitresses, a doctorate in the subject matter. That's bush. Put those details on a handout sheet and get down to the effective essentials of your talk. The mind can only take small chunks of information, and once you're gone, the audience will be hard-pressed to remember anything you said. However, they'll remember the way you said it forever.

3. Don't Bluff or Wing It

All effective presentations, even the impromptu meetings, are grounded in preparation and substance. Don't bluff, don't lie, don't wing it. If you're caught without the facts, say so.

4. The Fear Cure: Preparation

Most of us are not clinically phobic. Our anxiety won't escalate all the way to raw panic. Fear is a fuel that can be turned into power on the podium. The old real estate adage about location, location, location applies to prespeech jitters. Preparation, preparation, preparation will destroy fear.

8

5. Keep Focused on the Material as You Speak

If you start listening to yourself and evaluating your performance while you are speaking, you will lose concentration and, like a high-wire performer who looks down, fall. Instead, concentrate sharply on what you're saying as you're saying it. Your delivery will improve a hundredfold.

6. Don't Read from a Prepared Text

It sounds wooden.

7. Stay Within Your Allotted Time

A five-minute talk is not a ten-minute talk. Always know how much material you've got, and prepare on the short side of the limit. If you're told that you weren't up there long enough, you've done a wonderful job.

8. Humor: When In Doubt, Don't

You only have to go down the tubes once to know that humor isn't for everyone. Humor is one of the great loaded guns in public speaking. Unless you're pretty sure you can pull it off, let your competitor experiment with schtick. Let's face it, CEOs and senior VPs are not loaded with laughs.

9. Pause Before You Speak

Always take a few seconds to anchor yourself, put your notes in order, and get the feel of the audience before you begin to talk. You'll project control.

10. Act Confident

A funny thing happens when you act confident. They believe you. They laugh in the right places, lean forward, take notes, and nod as you speak. Now, confidence starts to shine through you, slowly at first, then at full speed. The longer you're up there, the better you'll feel, but you might have to do some acting when you first begin your talk.

INSTANT REVIEW

BASIC TRAINING

1. Know your introduction and conclusion cold.
2. Don't overexplain; put the details on a handout sheet.
3. Don't wing it.
4. Preparation: the fear cure.
5. Keep focused on the material; don't monitor youself as you speak.
6. Don't read your speech.
7. Stay within your allotted time.
8. Humor: when in doubt, don't.
9. Always pause before you speak.
10. Confidence is an acting job.

3

AN
AUDIENCE
ANALYSIS
CHECKLIST

BEFORE you prepare your talk, think about your audience. Are you talking to senior vice presidents in your own company, or a mixed bag from the whole industry? Will there be other speakers? A Q&A? What is the seating arrangement? The following checklist will eliminate some of the guesswork.

1. Why Are They There?

What's the deal here? Is there some common social or occupational bond that brings them to hear you? Is this a rote political event in the company? Who will need the information and who will not?

2. What Is Their Level of Knowledge About Your Topic?

Have a firm idea of what you want to cover, how much you realistically think they can absorb, and how much you'll need for the handout sheet.

3. What Is the Proportion of Women to Men?

The better you can visualize all factors in your audience, the easier the preparation. A woman addressing the last vestiges of a company's old-boy network should prepare her talk with those faces in mind. A man talking to a group of women should be similarly influenced.

4. What Is the Average Age of the Audience?

We're all creatures of our generation. Executives in their fifties, sixties, or seventies will have a different outlook on things and will interpret your material differently from thirty-year-olds. Age matters a lot.

5. What Attitudes and Prejudices Does the Audience Have About Your Topic?

Finance people like numbers. Personnel executives think of people slots and the cost of filling them. Everyone in your audience will evaluate your presentation in terms of his or her own corporate agenda.

6. What Is the Economic Level of Your Audience?

7. What Are Their Common Corporate Problems?

Does everyone in the room have to put up with a new computer system right after they got used to last year's new computer system? Did the CEO retire, leaving them with a lot of uncertainty? Their problems concern them constantly, and should concern you as you prepare your talk.

8. What Is the Physical Layout of the Room?

Preparation goes a lot smoother when you have some advance idea of the surroundings in which you'll give your talk.

9. Is There a Q&A? If So, for How Long?

Pace and prepare yourself for a question and answer session even if you have been told there will not be one. They have a way of popping up.

13

INSTANT REVIEW

AN AUDIENCE ANALYSIS CHECKLIST

1. Why are they there?
2. What is their level of knowledge about your topic?
3. What is the proportion of women to men?
4. What is the average age of the audience?
5. What attitudes and prejudices does the audience have about your topic?
6. What is the economic level of your audience?
7. What are the common corporate problems?
8. What is the layout of the room?
9. Will there be a Q&A?

4

THE
FAST WAY
TO WRITE
YOUR TALK

HE PRESENTATION writes itself when your notes are lean and placed in a sequence that makes sense to you. Don't overcomplicate the process. "Writing" might be talking through the facts instead of committing them to paper. To avoid the common pitfall of spending precious preparation time doing and redoing the introduction until there's no time for the main body and conclusion, try the following seven steps.

1. Jot It Down

Ideas rarely flow predictably. You might get the best brainstorm of the day in the shower, or as you drive to work. Keep a small notebook, micro cassette recorder, or an index card within reach; when an idea visits, capture it.

2. Make Yourself Write Down Everything You Think Belongs in Your Talk in One Single Session

It matters not whether you scribble, type, or write in whole sentences. Take an hour or less to get everything on paper. Pay no attention to form, order, or style. Just get it down.

3. Transfer Your Notes to Cards

Don't be bashful about using a lot of cards at this point. You'll trim later. *Talk* the speech through as if you're having a conversation with a friend in a bar. Don't write out any text yet. Business presentations call for just facts and their illustrations, so be prepared to throw a lot away. For now, just get the feel of the information and the cards.

4. Arrange the Cards in an Order That Makes Sense

You may not have written a single complete sentence at this point, but you already have your talk, however rough. Now put the cards in order and begin to trim away the information that is not pertinent to your topic.

16

5. Sculpt the Language

Your introduction and conclusion, though delivered from notes, require the most precision—and possibly the only real writing you'll do for most presentations. You have to know them as well as your own name. Choose your words and phrases carefully for maximum impact (see Chapter 9).

6. Develop a Rehearsal Outline

Now you have to do some serious cutting, working your information into the three basic parts of a talk: introduction, main body, conclusion. Use legal-size paper, plain bond, index cards, or any format you find comfortable. The rehearsal outline is an option, even a luxury, on many short-notice presentations. It serves as your out-of-town tryout so you can find out what works.

7. Shift Your Information to a Skeletal Outline

The skeletal outline is your final presentation road map. It should be a lean document that permits you to make eye contact with your audience. The information should serve only as a *reminder* of where you should be. The rest should be in your head. For example:

UNDERGROUND ECONOMY HITS ALL OF US IN POCKET

GOVT LOSES 90 BILLION; YOU LOSE (AT 100K) A CLEAR TWENTY THOU THIS YEAR

DATES BACK TO DEPRESSION

COURTS CLOGGED, ENFORCEMENT NIL

FOOD SERVICE INDUSTRY SEVERELY HIT BY UNDERGROUND ECONOMY

17

INSTANT REVIEW

SEVEN STEPS
TO WRITING YOUR TALK

1. Jot it down.
2. Write everything down in one single session.
3. Transfer notes to cards; talk it through.
4. Arrange cards in an order that makes sense to you.
5. Sculpt the language, especially the intro and conclusion.
6. Develop a detailed rehearsal outline.
7. Shift notes to a spare, skeletal outline.

5

THE ROOM-GRABBING INTRODUCTION

AS THE INTRO GOES, so goes the talk. Get them up front and they'll be with you for the whole ride. However, many factors beyond our control influence our first few minutes on stage. If you follow an exceptionally good speaker, or are the last to speak after a whole day of presentations in an overheated room, there isn't much that will work.

For the most part, though, you can assume you have them for the first minute or two. This chapter shows you

19

the pieces of a good intro and how to use them for maximum impact.

An introduction has to do five things:

1. **Command their attention**
2. **Connect for a one-to-one relationship**
3. **Establish your credibility as a speaker**
4. **Present your central theme emphatically**
5. **State your view of the central theme**

HOW TO COMMAND
THEIR ATTENTION

We are emotional creatures despite our veneer of accomplishment and education. We're always greedy children who want to know what's in it for us at all times. Place yourself in the audience as you prepare your intro. What would you want from you? Here are six ways to command audience attention at the top.

1. The Captivating Statement

"In 1975, eleven people invested ten thousand dollars apiece in my company. Last year, they became millionaires."

The captivating statement should jolt, rather than shock, the audience, for the main body of your delivery can't live up to a promise of sensationalism in the intro. The statement should press gently on the nerves, implying a near miss one way or the other; either something

20

wonderful happened to someone that could have happened to them, or they were fortunate enough to miss getting shafted. Sometimes you can take them on a thrill ride:

"If you invested ten thousand dollars with me in 1975, I'd have lost it all for you by 1980. . . . (Pause) And offered it back to you with a little interest in 1981. . . . (Pause) And if you went against the advice of all your sane friends and stayed with me, I'd have made you a millionaire this year."

Most captivating statements do the job in a single declarative sentence:

"Nine of us in this room will earn more than a million dollars a year by 1991."

2. The Statistical Display

The statistical display combines numbers with their human applications to grab attention:

"Last Christmas, 31,000 assembly-line workers in this state were able to flll their kids' stockings because there was plenty of work. All but 2,500 of those 31,000 workers remain unemployed today, and thanks to the governor, they will be joined by another 10,000 or more next Christmas Eve. I employ 440 people that I can no longer afford because of the capital equipment tax. I'm leaving, too. Merry Christmas, Governor."

21

3. Provocative Questions

Provocative questions, rhetorical or direct, wake an audience up:

For example: "Anyone here interested in an extra thousand a week, no strings attached?"

Or, "What does the color red have to do with employee productivity?"

Or, "If I told you that you wouldn't have to pay a dime for your children's education, what name would you call me?"

4. Quotations

> *"Let us all be happy to live within our means, even if we have to borrow the money to do it."*
> —CHARLES FARRAR BROWNE

> *"There was never a war of arms that was not merely the extension of a preceding war of commerce grown fiercer until the weapons of commerce seemed no longer significantly deadly."*
> —HUGH L. JOHNSON

A quotation takes the listener directly into the central theme of the talk. It can be effective anywhere in the text, so long as it is not overused.

5. Humor

Humor is one of the more common devices for making a one-to-one connection with an audience. But it should come in the form of a contextual quip or a bit of anchoring wit, rather than a joke: "First, I want to congratulate George Bennett on his success in cutting travel costs for management people. If any of you need more bus tokens, see me at lunch."

A good joke is grounded in taste and your confidence that the audience will get the gag. So, as we have stated, if you're even remotely in doubt, use another device.

6. Visual Attention Grabbers

Technical presentations lend themselves best to visual drama in the introduction. If you're demonstrating the danger of a combustible chemical, or the brightness of halogen versus fluorescent lighting, a demonstration can perk them right up and get you off to a great start. The problem, of course, is that visuals can be stagey.

MAKE A ONE-TO-ONE CONNECTION IN YOUR INTRODUCTION

Never broadcast. *Talk* to your audience as if you're talking to one person. You're just one individual sitting down with another to talk this thing out. Public speaking is probably better termed "public talking." Here are five strategies for making that one-to-one connection.

1. Be Yourself

You were asked to speak because someone thinks you've got something important to say. Congratulations. Let the audience see the real you.

2. Use Your Own Stories

Stories—your stories—that relate to the central theme require no dazzle or joke-telling ability. A direct personal experience with the topic told in a straightforward manner usually goes much further than theatrics:

"A lot of you might feel that biomedical engineering is some kind of mutation to family life as we know it. I understand that position because, until I joined the company, I felt the same way. Not only did I feel that the technology sounded the death knell for family life, but I thought it dangerous for every organism on the phylogenetic scale. Let me tell you why I no longer see things that way."

You're talking *to* them.

3. Address Their Needs in Your Intro

Once they buy you, there is plenty of time to address your own problems and ideas. In the introduction, address *their* problems and needs.

4. Maximize the Moment Right After You've Been Introduced

Between the moderator's glowing introduction and the opening phrase of your intro is a moment of anticipation. The audience is saying, "Who is this?" It's the perfect time to lean into them a bit and draw them to you. You might do it formally: "Thank you very much, Jane Walmsley. Jane showed me the facility this morning and I'm very impressed."

Or, informally: "Thanks, Bob. I love Chicago. I wasn't happy to see what the Bears did to the Giants last week, but it's always great to be back."

But YOU DON'T HAVE TO BE FUNNY. A simple acknowledgment of some commonality will serve as a connector that sells you before your introduction.

5. The Show of Hands

Asking an audience how many present ever did this, or saw that, will loosen them up, add to your own information about them, and establish a link. It makes the conversation more intimate.

THE ROOM-GRABBING INTRODUCTION

1. Commands attention
2. Connects for a one-to-one relationship
3. Establishes your credibility as a speaker
4. Presents your central theme emphatically
5. States your view of the central theme

SIX WAYS TO GRAB ATTENTION
IN AN INTRODUCTION

1. The captivating statement
2. The statistical display
3. Provocative questions
4. Quotations
5. Humor
6. Visual attention grabbers

FIVE WAYS TO MAKE
A ONE-TO-ONE CONNECTION
WITH YOUR AUDIENCE

1. Be yourself
2. Use your best stories
3. Address their needs
4. Maximize the moment right after the moderator intro-
   duces you
5. Use a show of hands

HOW TO USE THE INTRODUCTION FOR MAXIMUM IMPACT

Now that we've shown you the pieces of a room-grabbing introduction, it's time to give you the tips you need to use your intro properly.

There are four reasons why mastery of the intro assures the seizing, and keeping, of an audience's attention.

1. When You Take Over at the Top of Your Presentation, the Rest Is Simple

Get them in the first few minutes and they'll follow you anywhere. A good intro will cover a multitude of content and delivery sins.

2. A Strong Intro Highlights Your Natural Leadership Ability

In fact, you might even get more leadership credit than you deserve when senior management people, who barely noticed you in the halls, watch you walk to the front of the room and take command.

3. A Great Intro Deals a Lethal Blow to Nervousness

Do well at the top and, assuming you are well prepared, anxiety transforms itself into excitement and enthusiasm in your delivery. You won't be tentative for the rest of the presentation.

27

4. In a Great Introduction, Your Personal Style Becomes an Asset

If a strong, honest intro is delivered in a low-key manner, you will be remembered as subtle and in complete control. With a vibrant, enthusiastic delivery, you will be perceived as even more so. So long as you are direct, concise, and look in control, there is no right or wrong style.

Here are the "Big Do's" of an effective introduction.

1. Converse at All Times

The whole tone of your speech should be exactly as if you were speaking to a friend. Whether you address a single imaginary person (a delivery technique you'll hear more about in Chapter 16) or develop your own system, the language you choose should fit you like a glove. If you don't use words in conversation, don't use them in meetings or on the podium.

2. Be Solution-Oriented

A businesslike, solution-oriented tone in your introduction establishes instant credibility: "There are three ways for us to enter the market, and I see only one of those paths as viable without a major acquisition."

3. Be Precise

Credibility and precision are the same thing in a business presentation. Pack your talk with real information and leave suppositions or generalities at home.

28

Vague: "Legions of workers have benefited from the new medical coverage since we inaugurated it eighteen or so months ago."

Precise: "We inaugurated this program in January of 1986 and have since insured 4,902 employees in our product development division. There have been 51 claims for minor injuries, 14 major trauma injuries, and three hospital visits of more than a week's duration. All claims were settled without legal contest."

4. Be Brief

An introduction tells the audience what they're going to hear in a few quick statements. Watch a powerful person in a meeting. He or she comes right to the point, wasting very little time on banter. A long statement is weak. A short statement is strong.

Don't say: "I've given considerable thought to the implications of that problem, bearing in mind its many ramifications, and how others in this room may feel about it. I would have to say it is totally untenable."

Say: "I disagree."

The Big Don'ts are bigger in the introduction than in any part of the speech.

1. The Biggest Don't:
Don't Put Too Much Pressure on Your Intro

An introduction is a seduction. You can't just stampede your way to success with it. You can only put so much pressure on your delivery; if you overdo it, you'll find yourself waiting for a joke to go over, or for a reaction to your carefully timed, shocking first sentence. When none of it happens, as it often doesn't for ten

29

thousand reasons having nothing to do with you, you'll get thrown and stumble through the rest of the talk.

You can't preach, educate, or topple your audience with detail. You can't dazzle with your brilliance yet, because they haven't bought you.

2. *Never Apologize*

Do not sell off your credibility with an apology or equivocation.

Don't Say: "I'm not really a specialist in cost accounting, but I'll muddle through as best I can."

Say: "In my law practice, I constantly work with cost accountants, and they hate tax-deferred investments for three reasons."

If you're up there, someone thinks you have the authority to run the show. You have to think so, too.

3. *Don't Make Promises in the Introduction That Can't Be Delivered in the Main Body*

You should never be so provocative, so flamboyant, or so dynamic that you're making an offer you can't back up in the talk: "During the next thirty minutes, I will change the way you look at your life."

4. *Don't Force a Commonality That Does Not Exist*

If you don't have a lot in common with your audience, that's all right. Don't stretch for some piece of your ancestry or background that you think shows you to be sensitive to their problems. If you're in management and they're union, you won't really buy points by saying that your dad drove trucks the semester he dropped out of Harvard.

30

5. *Don't Hedge*

Don't make statements like:

"I'd have to double check those figures, but . . ."

"I'm not entirely sure of this, but . . ."

"Well, it could go entirely the other way, and I'm not saying I entirely disagree, but . . ."

State what you mean. We *know* there are two sides to an issue. We want to hear your side.

An exception to the don't hedge rule is when you take a question from the audience, especially when it is unrelated to your central theme.

6. *Don't Be Too Impressed by Your Audience*

Don't fawn. It doesn't win you any votes.

Don't say: "I'm intimidated to be in the room with such a distinguished group."

Say: "I'm honored to be here."

7. *Don't Use Buzz Words and Trendy Language*

You'll look like you're trying too hard.

INSTANT REVIEW

HOW TO USE THE INTRODUCTION
FOR MAXIMUM IMPACT

Four reasons why mastery of the intro assures
audience attention:

1. When you take over at the top, they buy you all the way through.
2. A strong intro showcases your natural leadership abilities.
3. A great intro deals a lethal blow to nervousness.
4. In a great intro, personal style becomes an asset.

The four Do's of an effective intro:

1. Converse at all times
2. Be solution-oriented
3. Be precise
4. Be brief

The seven Don'ts:

1. Don't put too much pressure on the intro.
2. Never apologize.
3. Don't make promises you can't deliver.
4. Don't force a commonality that does not exist.
5. Don't hedge.
6. Don't be too impressed by your audience.
7. Don't use buzz words and trendy language.

6

THE
MAIN BODY

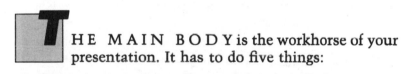

THE MAIN BODY is the workhorse of your presentation. It has to do five things:

1. Sustain the audience's interest
2. Follow a logical order
3. Sound the theme music: follow a common central thread
4. Provide variations in pace
5. Offer smooth transitions from subject to subject

33

THREE WAYS TO SUSTAIN THE AUDIENCE'S INTEREST WHEN YOU GET TO THE MAIN BODY

1. **Believe in your material**
2. **Don't waste time**
3. **Don't rely too heavily on visuals or gimmicks**

You, and not your data, hold the audience's attention. You can't blow it when you present a direct, enthusiastic summation of your material. They might believe it or they might think it's a crock, but if *you* believe it, they'll respect you.

Having gotten their attention in the introduction, there is little to do but pack the main body with substance. Attention will waver, especially if you're up there for a while, but don't worry. They'll come back if your energy is up.

All executives have an alarm that serves as an early warning system for bluff, fill, and other excess verbiage. They never have enough time, and they will become hostile if you are not direct.

Too many corporate speakers drone on with slides, flip charts, videos, and other visuals. While we acknowledge the value of these devices, our position is do without them whenever possible. Visuals are Valium to your momentum.

34

TWO PATHS FOR MAINTAINING A LOGICAL ORDER IN YOUR MAIN BODY

Once you've introduced your central theme, lay out your logic like a map, tell them where you're going. Here are two maps for getting to the conclusion smoothly.

1. The Subject Path

The subject path breaks the topic itself into its key components—often, three parts:

"The bankruptcy occurred for three key reasons. The company was undercapitalized, it failed to expand on time, and the management structure was top heavy with sales people."

2. The Chronological Path

The chronological path follows a time line through a presentation where one event must precede another in order to make sense:

"Retooling for underground pipe manufacture will first require the shutting down of the Altoona plant. Once we decide to do that, personnel will make recommendations on which employees we should lay off. . . ."

SOUNDING THE THEME MUSIC

Throughout your talk, it's a good idea to remind the audience of your central theme:

35

"There are two *more* reasons why workers who smoke need their own place to do so."

"Loss of central control is *another* solid argument against divestiture."

VARY YOUR PACE

Break it up. Every ten or fifteen minutes, drop the formality, inject a personal anecdote, talk to a few people in the audience. In a long talk, your listeners need a break somewhere between fifty and seventy-five minutes.

BUILDING TRANSITIONS

Transitions are rivets in your main body. They provide a seamless bond from one piece to another, always reminding audiences of the central theme. Here are seven workable transitions; the first four are verbal, the last three nonverbal.

1. Reiterate Your Central Theme

"Computer security in the workplace requires more than staff. It requires an attitude change."

2. Personal Anecdote as Transition

Your own experiences are as refreshing and welcome in the main body as any other piece of the talk. A personal experience illustrates your point:

36

"Three years ago, I had to find a new way to warehouse our overstock."

3. Summarize the Points You've Covered

"We've seen how inattention to computer security affects management-employee relationships, research and development costs, and middle management morale. Now we have arrived at the pivotal strain: the effects of computer crime on the individual office worker."

4. Transitional Phrases

Uso short words of phrases to move from one subtopic to another:

"*Let's sum* up the results of the survey."

"*However*, the story doesn't end there."

"*Continuing* with our discussion on target marketing . . ."

"*Inevitably*, there are complications."

"*Thus far*, we've seen how . . ."

5. Pause

Take three seconds before continuing. When you resume speaking, your voice will signal another idea.

37

6. Use a Piece of Stage Business to Change Topics

Take a sip of water, turn partly to another sector of the audience, shift eye contact, and so on.

7. Use Body Language to Indicate a New Subject

Shift your weight, change your gestures, walk to the side of the podium, or otherwise signal the next topic.

THE MAIN BODY

The main body must:

1. Sustain the audience's interest
2. Follow a logical order
3. Sound the theme music
4. Offer variations in pace
5. Provide smooth transitions from subject to subject

Three ways to sustain interest:

1. Believe in your material
2. Don't waste time
3. Don't rely on visuals or gimmicks

Two paths for keeping the main body on a logical course

1. Subject Path: breaks topic into its key components
2. Chronological Path: follows a time line through a presentation where one event must precede another in order to make sense

Seven workable transitions:

1. Reiterate your central theme
2. Use personal anecdote as transition
3. Summarize the points you've made thus far
4. Use transitional phrases
5. Pause
6. Use a piece of stage business
7. Use body language to indicate a new topic

7

THE CONCLUSION: YOUR BIG FINISH

THE CONCLUSION is your final chance to leave an impression. It has to be big—and small. It says nothing new, it is always brief, and it carries the bonus of elevated audience attention. A conclusion should:

1. Signal the End of the Talk

Tell them you're ending, and they'll be all yours. Even the weakest tip-off, "In conclusion," or one of its bland variations, snaps people awake. However, you don't have to use words to send the signal. A note of finality in your voice works just as well.

2. Briefly Summarize Your Main Points

Brevity is imperative here. Once you've told them you're wrapping up, they rightfully expect you to leave the platform.

3. Reiterate Your Central Theme

One or two notes of theme music is more than enough.

4. Convey a Tone of Optimism

It's not written in cement, but a conclusion usually puts the best face on a situation and points to an optimistic future, even if things aren't so great right now.

5. Offer a Final Salutation

The final salutation tells them you're through and thanks them for the courtesy of listening. It should be brief and classy. Five workable signals to the conclusion are:

1. "Let me leave you with . . ."
2. "Finally . . ."
3. "Before I finish, I'm reminded of . . ."
4. "I'll end with . . ."
5. "One final thought . . ."

THREE EXAMPLES OF
BRIEF (FIVE- TO FIFTEEN-SECOND)
SUMMATIONS

"To remain competitive, we must *recognize the global marketplace as the future of American manufacturing, educate ourselves in the political structure of the newly industrialized nations,* and *retool for these profit centers of the twenty-first century.*"

"Our profligate spending in the 1980s will be paid for with *a decline in consumer credit, steep taxes on luxury items,* and *a cap on the services we can reasonably expect our government to provide.*"

"The expansion, then, is threefold. *Open the territory to new franchises, reduce construction costs by 30 percent per unit,* and *eliminate seven unprofitable items from our product line.*"

THREE REITERATIONS OF THE MAIN THEME

"When we recognize the buried treasure in the international marketplace . . ."

"It's not impossible to curb our spending."

"Expansion, not cutbacks, is the key to our immediate growth."

43

TONES OF OPTIMISM

"We've been through tough times and they're not over yet, but *we have a long tradition of turning adversity into gold. We won't just prevail. We will win big.*"

"As we have seen, the eighties have also produced the most *promising explosion of entrepreneurial innovation since the industrial revolution. I salute the thousands of small businesses that demonstrate the power of our economy.*"

FINAL SALUTATION TIPS

The final salutation is the punctuation mark of your presentation, the last thing they hear you say. There's nothing wrong with a genuine, "Thank you very much," but it's nicer to make a small acknowledgment of the city, someone who was especially helpful, or just the courtesy of their attention.

"Thank you for making my stay in Phoenix so special."

"I've enjoyed working with you and already look forward to my next visit to Consolidated."

"I really enjoyed it here. Thank you."

"Thank you all very much. I look forward to seeing many of you at the home office."

PUTTING IT TOGETHER

Signal to the Conclusion: "To sum up . . ."

Brief Summary of Main Points: "The profligate spending in the 1980s will be paid for three ways. There will be less consumer spending, higher taxes on luxury items, and fewer services that we can reasonably expect from our government."

Sound Theme Music: "We spent too much. We can't change that."

Note of Optimism: "However, the eighties have also seen the rise of the most promising explosion of innovative entrepreneurialism since the Industrial Revolution. I salute these new entrepreneurs who demonstrate the continuing power of our economy, who prove by their numbers and success that American business is stronger than the momentary frailties of our political system."

Final Salutation: "I want to thank all of you at Davco for making my stay in Dallas so pleasant. Continued success to a first-rate company."

ADDITIONAL TIPS FOR YOUR CONCLUSION

1. Conclusions are always short. If you find yours going on too long, shorten it.
2. Conclusions do not introduce new concepts.
3. When possible, conclusions should relate back to a thought presented in the introduction:
   "I went back to that mattress factory and found Oscar still at his machine twenty-five years later."

45

"When we started, I said there were four reasons to purchase gold this year."

"Returning to Socrates . . ."

5. Use your most muscular language at the end of the talk: "Vote. That is all we ask."

INSTANT REVIEW

THE CONCLUSION

A conclusion should:

1. Signal the end of the talk
2. Briefly summarize your main points
3. Reiterate your central theme
4. Convey an optimistic tone
5. Offer a final salutation
6. Be short
7. Relate back to introduction whenever possible
8. Use your most muscular language

8

HIGH
IMPACT
LANGUAGE:
CHOOSING WORDS
WITH CLOUT

SUCCESSFUL PEOPLE convey precision and force when they speak. Watch the CEO. His words are probably spare and packed with information. You need no dictionary or thesaurus to understand his message. His talk is never the jargon-laden drudge of the specialist—that's for middle managers. CEO talk is not full of imagery and rich phraseology—that's too vague. There are no long-distance detours to spare someone's feelings—that's for the shrinks. With top management people, the point is right out front and usually demands immediate action.

As you prepare your presentation, sculpt your language into the shape of plain English. Empty it of long-windedness. Write for the ear. Homer was a singer. Shakespeare was an actor. Mark Twain swatted big words like so many flies and made a pretty good living without them—you will, too.

The Magic Monosyllable

The most forceful words in our language are monosyllabic: God, love, fight, hate, help, hurt. The most provocative emotion you can convey is packaged in a four-letter word. When you bang your thumb with a hammer, what word comes right out? If you get cut off by some jerk at an intersection and nearly lose your front end, do you want to *discuss* the matter? The right word is always there in a syllable.

Leaders have known this for centuries:

> *"I have a dream."*
> —MARTIN LUTHER KING

> *"Give us the tools and we will do the job."*
> —WINSTON CHURCHILL

> *"Ask not what your country can do for you . . ."*
> —JOHN F. KENNEDY

48

We fight and *die* with monosyllabic inspiration:

Keep America free.

Loose lips sink ships.

War is hell.

Buy bonds.

The war to end all wars.

Here are six high impact language strategies:

1. Put Your Imprint on Your Position with a Personal Stand

Show your belief in what you say by coming forward and putting yourself on the line:

Low Impact: "Many in the company want to see a re-evaluation."

High Impact: "I say we reevaluate."

Low Impact: "It could be argued that there are other solutions."

High Impact: "*My* reaction is that there are other solutions and *I'll* tell you what they are."

2. Euphemisms Are Low Impact

Don't Say: "members of *minority groups* might object."

Say: "*Black people* won't like it at all."

Don't Say: "Their *financial assets* are *dwindling*."

Say: "They're running out of money."

49

3. Put Absolute Words and Phrases Into Your Language

Adding "all" to a phrase frequently strengthens it:
Low Impact: "Our employees are factory-trained."
High Impact: "All our employees are factory-trained."
"Really should" is low impact: "You really should get it done fast."
"Should" carries clout: "You should get it done fast."

4. Abbreviations Are Low Impact

"The HEW, the FCC, and the NAB are cooperating with the SEC in its investigation."
Instead, spell it out: "The Department of Health, Education and Welfare, the Federal Communications Commission, and the National Association of Broadcasters are cooperating with the Securities and Exchange Commission in its investigation."

Remember: Jargon is low impact unless everyone in the room uses the terminology every day. Even then, think twice before using esoteric language in a presentation.

5. Use the Active Voice

Passive (low impact) voice: "The referendum will be voted upon by the executive council."
Active (high impact) voice: "The executive council will take a vote on the referendum."

6. Use Softeners Sparingly

In a meeting, where power often flows from chair to chair, diplomacy might call for padding your position with a softener, such as, "It seems to me that . . ." In a presentation, your goal should be to deliver an equivocation-free communication. That leaves out hundreds of insurance phrases in the English language, such as:

"I could be mistaken but . . ."

"I'll double check my facts, but . . ."

"Is it me or did I observe . . ."

"I know you might interpret this as . . ."

"It seems to me that . . ."

"Time may prove me wrong, of course, but . . ."

"In my opinion . . ."

"It is the judgment of many, including myself, that . . ."

7. Weed Out Platitudes and Generalities

Avoid such phrases as:

Facing an important challenge

Conquering the future

Welcoming an opportunity

Rising to the occasion

51

Forging ahead

Seeing not problems, but opportunities

A company is only as good as its people

8. Use Contrast

"I am forced every month to *lie* to the accounting department in order to get reimbursed for an *honest* business lunch with a colleague."

"I would rather be a *champion* production manager than a *mediocre* vice president of manufacturing."

"There was once *sloth*, now there is *ambition*. There was once *discontent*, now there is *harmony*. There was once *anger*, now there is *joy*. There was once *apathy*, now there is *pride*."

9. Repeat for Emphasis

"There are three things to remember about retailing: location, *location*, and LOCATION!"

10. Nurturing Words Are Weak

The Sensitive Seventies are long gone and so is all that talk about business with a moral mission. Not that you have to get up there and act like you're personally kicking Khaddafi in the groin as you speak, but words and phrases such as "sensitivity," "human potential," "getting in touch with," "reassure," "feed," "nurture," "nonthreatening," and "feelings" carry a connotation of public sector babble.

52

11. Diminutives Insult

A "nice little facility" or a "sharp little operation" won't score you any points with your audience.

PHRASES WITH TOO MANY WORDS	
LOW IMPACT	HIGH IMPACT
In point of fact	In fact
A total of ____	(Just give the number)
To be perfectly honest	(Nothing; what were you
candid	before this?)
frank	
To tell you the truth	(Skip the phrase)
As a matter of fact	In fact (or delete)
Under the present circumstances	Currently
When you check into the facts	When you look closer
Be that as it may	But
Long in duration	Long
Suffice to say	(Delete)
At the present time	Now
As you are aware	(Delete unless you're saving some dolt embarrassment)
As you may already know	You may have heard
Advance planning	Plans, Planning
Are in agreement with	Agree

LOW IMPACT	HIGH IMPACT
Due to the fact that	Because
Oddly enough	Oddly
Is fully operational	Works well
In close proximity to	Near
Predicated upon	Based on
Close personal friend	Friend
With regard to	Regarding
Thusly	Thus
Of sufficient magnitude	Big enough
Until such time as	Until
Impact on	Affect
Consensus of opinion	Agreement
The body of work	The work
For all practical purposes	(Delete)
A point well taken	A good point
In the event of	If
End result	Result
Each and every one	Each
In the course of	During
Give credence to	Believe
Never before or since	Never

INSTANT REVIEW

HIGH IMPACT LANGUAGE

1. Keep language informational and spare.
2. Take a personal stand.
3. Euphemisms are low impact.
4. Use absolutes.
5. Don't use abbreviations.
6. Use the active voice.
7. Avoid softeners.
8. Weed out platitudes and generalities.
9. Use contrast.
10. Repeat for emphasis.
11. Nurturing words are weak.
12. Diminutives insult.

9

THE
BODY
LANGUAGE
OF THE
TAKE-CHARGE
SPEAKER

BODY LANGUAGE has a fifty-thousand-year evolutionary jump on the spoken word. We can read a person by watching his or her gestures. Long before the talk shows of the early 1970s added the phrase to our language, Darwin observed that all limbed animals cross their arms when they perceive a threat.

But don't take Darwin's word for it. Watch the people at a medical center. You can spot a doctor across a parking lot long before you see a name plate, stethoscope, or sur-

57

gical scrubs. Physicians at work move with the authority of monarchs.

When you walk to the speaker's position, your body should signal your authority. While we defer to more comprehensive texts and classroom instruction for a thorough indoctrination, a short description of the nine tips for taking over follows.

1. Walk in Even, Deliberate Steps Toward Your Speaking Position

Move with the grace of a millionaire inspecting his grounds. Move evenly, as if you do this sort of thing every day.

2. Stand with Your Weight Evenly Distributed on Both Feet

Plant your feet in imaginary buckets of cement when you reach the podium. Don't shift from one foot to the other. Stand squarely.

3. Pause Before You Speak

You send signals of nervousness or insecurity when you launch right into a talk. Take five seconds to settle in, plant your feet, adjust the mike, and look directly at the audience.

4. As You Deliver, Move Your Whole Body Toward Various Sections of the Room

Most people try to connect with the audience simply by turning their heads from one part of the room to another as they speak.

58

This is not enough. Go all the way. Move your whole upper torso two or three times as you sweep the room.

5. Feel Free to Walk Around a Little During a Long Talk

If you're up there a while, move out of those cement buckets, just don't dart or do it too often. Pacing, usually done in little steps, is low impact. A deliberate walk to the front or side of the podium to punctuate a key change of pace is high impact.

6. Jerky, Uneven Movement Is Low Impact

Those with little chance of claiming a room move in uneven, fidgety spurts that beg to be interrupted. There is a constant halfway effort at one gesture, followed by another small move, then another. These people never seem relaxed.

7. High Impact Speakers Complete Their Gestures

You never have to wonder if a speaker is in control. You know by his gestures. A hand sweeps right up and punctuates a point. It completes its cycle.

8. The High Impact Pace Is Brisk But Relaxed

You're always going somewhere and the room knows it. Your pace is soothing to them because they know you're at the controls. However, you are never, never hurried. Hurried is low impact.

59

9. Your Eyes Set the Pace

Your eyes are the pace car at the body language Indy. The rest of your gestures should merely confirm what your eyes say. If it is off, the rest of the body language won't be much help.

EYE CONTACT

Good eye contact with your audience is not merely an imperative in a business speech, it is your ticket to credibility. You should use your eyes to underscore your points, to challenge, amuse, and drive home your main points with the explosive crackle of a jackhammer.

An old speaking adage holds that you should look just above the heads of the audience to avoid the intimidation of direct contact. Wrong! Such a bad habit is akin to learning to type with your thumbs. You'll get good only when you learn to make a crisp, compelling connection with your audience through eye contact.

Look directly at them except for brief breaks when you can refer to your topic outline. Say hello to someone on the left with eyes that blaze with conviction. Feel the snap of rapport, move down or to the right and say hello to someone else for a second. Eye contact is achieved as follows:

1. During the Pause Before Your Intro, Make Your First Eye Contact

Don't just meet someone's gaze, COMMUNICATE. Your face should be honest, open, and unafraid of a smile. It all starts with your eyes.

2. As You Deliver Your Talk, Move from the Far Left to the Near Right in a Z Pattern

Any movement from left to right is fine, but remember that you have to connect with the front, middle, and back of the audience.

3. Don't Feel as If You Have to Stop at Every Face

Since you are elevated, the face you choose to greet with your eyes represents everyone in that sector of the audience.

4. Don't Stare

Eye contact is not a duel at dawn. Just say hi and move on after a couple of seconds.

INSTANT REVIEW

TAKE-CHARGE BODY LANGUAGE

1. Approach your speaking position in even, deliberate steps.
2. Stand with your weight evenly on both feet.
3. Pause before you speak.
4. Move your whole body toward various sections of the room.
5. Feel free to walk around a little during a long talk.
6. Jerky, uneven movement is low impact.
7. High impact speakers complete their gestures.
8. The high impact pace is brisk but relaxed.
9. Your eyes set the pace.

EYE CONTACT

1. Make your first eye contact during the pause before your intro.
2. Move from the far left to the near right as you deliver your talk.
3. Don't feel as if you have to stop at every face.
4. Don't stare.

10

JUST BEFORE
YOU
SPEAK

S THERE ANYTHING MORE ab-
surd than trying to *relax* before a big presentation? Forget that nonsense. If your body is pumping
adrenaline, your legs feel as if they're about to give way,
and your mouth is a dry lake bed, your emotions are in
place. You're ready to use that energy to turn lackluster
into blockbuster.

The following techniques will help you put the adrenaline to work on your behalf.

1. Don't Try to Fight Your Physiology

Own it. Stand still for a moment and feel the physical mani-festation of nerves—tight shoulders, legs, neck; chills; weakened knees; stomach aflutter. These sensations won't get out of control once you allow them to flow through you.

2. Focus on a Single Object for Thirty Seconds While Breathing Deeply

It might be a glass, a spoon, a pencil—anything in the room. Concentrate on every inch of that object as you breathe deeply. You'll be amazed at how much power you feel.

3. Place the Fist of One Hand into the Palm of the Other and Push for Ten Seconds

4. Plain Old Deep, Slow Breathing Is a Great Control Mechanism

Breathing alone, however, is way too passive. It needs focus. When you inhale, think "Iiiiiiin," when you exhale, it's "Ouuuuuuuuuuuut."

5. Crumble a Napkin or a Piece of Paper into the Palm of Your Hand and Squeeze as Hard as You Can for Five Seconds

64

6. Rub Your Hands Together Rapidly and Focus on the Build-up of Heat and Energy

As you do this (when no one is around, of course), think clearly about the positive aspects of your talk and visualize a successful result.

7. Take a Deep, Slow Breath as You Extend Your Arms Outward as Far as They Go

Stretch and repeat the exercise a few times.

8. Clench Both Fists Tightly and Punch Downward

Do this first with one hand, then the other. It will loosen you up considerably.

9. Tilt Your Head to the Left, Stretch, and Return to Your Normal Position

Now stretch to the right; repeat the motion until you're feeling in control.

10. Visualize Your Energy Level on a Scale from One to Ten

Take stock of where you feel you are at this minute, then raise the level a couple of notches.

There are thousands of de-stressing possibilities and most of them focus on a simple cycle of tensing, then

65

relaxing your body's muscles. If you can get into the habit of putting a few of these physiological tricks to work just before an important presentation, you'll become a much better speaker.

INSTANT REVIEW

JUST BEFORE YOU SPEAK

Experiment with tension/release until you develop the de-stressers that work for you. Choose from:

1. Don't fight the nervous energy.
2. Focus on a single object and breathe deeply.
3. Place the fist of one hand into the palm of the other and push.
4. Plain old deep, slow breathing is still a great trick but focus as you breathe.
5. Crumble a napkin or a piece of paper into your fist and squeeze.
6. Rub your hands together rapidly.
7. Take a deep, slow breath as you extend your arms outward a few times.
8. Clench both fists tightly and punch downward with one hand, then the other.
9. Tilt your head to the left, then to the right, and stretch.
10. Visualize your energy level on a scale and raise it a notch.

11

POWERVOICING

THE VOICE is the great untapped power resource of business communication. With very little practice, you can use it to get what you want. This chapter will show you how to use inflection to your advantage, make your voice deeper, breathe diaphragmatically for a more authoritative sound, and get rid of annoying vocal mannerisms, such as "uh," "uhm," and "you know."

Few of us mine the treasure of voice. One of nature's

cruelties is housing our vocal apparatus near the inner ear. We hear a much nicer voice than we project—that braying ass on the tape is someone else. You may not fall in love with your voice, but with this chapter's tips, you'll be able to use it better.

INFLECTION

The message of a spoken word or phrase is a matter of how you use volume to emphasize it:
"I want it done *today*."
"I *want* it done today."
The first sentence leaves very little doubt as to when the speaker expects the job done. The same task in the second sentence is inflected as an unlikely wish. Inflection reveals how we feel about the words we use.

UPWARD VERSUS DOWNWARD INFLECTION

Say "get." The word lends itself to an even, nonjudgmental inflection. Now pose it as a question: "Get?"
Say it with moderate conviction: *"Get."*
And as a command: "Get!"
When you posed "get" as a question, you were using upward inflection. When you hammered it with conviction and command, you were speaking with downward inflection.
Any word or phrase can be spoken with upward and downward inflection. Upward is tentative, as if you're

68

going for a question. Downward is authoritative. Practice reading aloud and underlining various words for emphasis and inflection:

"The stock market *showed early signs of* recovery *this morning, but analysts say it may be* weeks *before we feel the full effect of yesterday's plunge."*

Versus:

"The stock market showed early *signs of recovery* this morning, *but analysts say it may be weeks before we feel the* full effect *of yesterday's plunge."*

You can also practice single syllable words and bring them up and down the inflection scale.

Hi. (Faint)

Hi. (Conversational inflection)

Hi? (Tentative)

Hi. (Hearty)

HI! (Boisterous)

Use a tape recorder when you practice. Your speaking pattern is a trunk full of jagged bits and pieces of speech that you learned as you were growing up. Most people believe speech, once formed, is locked in stone. In fact, you can learn new speaking patterns with a little practice. Inflection is one of the most useful power tools of business communication.

69

PITCH

To lower the pitch of your voice:

1. Open Your Mouth Wider When You Speak

Your mouth is a natural resonating chamber that, when opened, brings the level of your voice down to a much more convincing pitch.

2. Practice by Alternating Your Normal Speaking Pitch with a Lower One

While the tape recorder is running, say "Aaaaaa-aaaaahhhhhhhh" in your normal speaking voice. Loosen up by taking three slow, deep breaths, then rolling your head around comfortably. Now open your mouth wider and say "Aaaaaaaaahhhhhhh" again. You'll hear the difference and your tape will confirm it.

Keep alternating tones; first, use your regular pitch, then open your mouth and hold a note on a deeper pitch.

3. Read Aloud at the Lower Pitch

4. Finally, Try It in Conversation on a Limited Basis

Eventually, your pitch will be more authoritative in conversation. Remember not to expect miracles. You've been speaking at the same pitch since you were a child, and you're not about to suddenly burst on the scene as some kind of conference room Pavarotti. Work slowly.

70

VOLUME

Powervoicing is not being loud. Very often, it's lowering the volume, so that those around you have to lean forward to hear. A few tips:

1. Practice Projecting Your Voice to the Far Corner of Various Rooms

Get someone to stand at the end of the room and throw your voice directly to that person *without* changing pitch. Try a small room first, then a larger room. You'll find that you shout and distort at first, but that is only a temporary condition. The overmodulation will soon be replaced by an even, controlled level that will forever serve you well in meetings.

2. Work on Lowering Your Voice

When you are away from the office, experiment with variations in volume; lower your voice to make a point and watch as friends move toward you. Increase your level to your normal volume range and lower it again.

3. Watch the Pros

Look at television with a new perspective; observe how talk show guests and comedians use volume for emphasis and timing.

The powerful person talks at an even volume, feeling free to summon higher or lower voice range when needed, but sparingly. People who talk too loud display the insecurity of someone afraid to be interrupted. If you're too soft-spoken, people will walk right

71

over you. Speak at an even level, and be very calculated about your use of the highs and lows.

BREATH CONTROL

Your voice rides on a column of air that rests on a foundation known as the *diaphragm*, the home base of powervoicing. You can find it by placing your palm just below the rib cage and above the navel. To speak from the diaphragm, you must first assess your posture.

When Standing for a Presentation: Practice the following position.

1. Place your feet shoulder-width apart and distribute your body weight *evenly* on both feet.

2. Keep your head raised to the eye level of someone your height.

3. Your chest is raised, and your stomach tucked in. This is not to say that you have to scrunch in a paunch. That's another exercise altogether. You're not covering your midriff, just bringing it to some kind of attention.

When Sitting for a Meeting: Take the following position.

1. Sit up straight. Most of us touch the back of the chair with the upper torso when the lower back should really be making the contact.

2. Place both feet on the floor and leave them there.

3. Place your hands together but don't lock them. You'll need them for gesturing.

72

DIAPHRAGMATIC BREATHING

Diaphragmatic breathing occurs when you fill your chest cavity with as much air as it can hold. If you can reach the diaphragm when you breathe, and open your mouth wide, your voice will increase its resonance.

1. Inhale

Place your hand on your abdomen and take a deep breath. If the stomach area pushes *outward*, you are breathing diaphragmatically. If it moves *inward*, you're running on a few less cylinders and depriving your voice of its power. Practice inhaling deeply and allowing your abdomen to move outward.

2. Exhale Totally

Force all the air you can out of the chest region; make sure that your abdominal muscles move *away* from the body.

3. Practice Inhaling and Exhaling as Deeply as Possible

Keep the abdominal muscles moving outwardly.

4. Open Your Mouth Wide and Say "Aaaaaaaaaahhhhhhhhhhhh"

You should find a deeper, fuller voice after a few tries.

73

HOW TO FIX SPEECH MANNERISMS

Speech mannerisms are nervous conversational habits such as "Uh," "Uhm," "You know," and "Like." They can also be nonverbal sounds, for example, an involuntary giggle, clearing your throat, or smacking your lips after every sentence.

The hardest part about kicking mannerisms is finding them. We don't hear our problems. Assuming you can find a mannerism, here are four tips for getting rid of it:

1. Write It on an Index Card and Carry the Card with You

If you have an "Uh" mannerism, write "Uh" on a card by itself. Look at it two or three times a day.

2. Tape Your Conversations

Keep a cassette recorder near the phone, or in some spot where you can reach over and turn it on as you talk. Let it run at various times for a few days before playing back your conversations. Then you'll know the extent of your difficulties with the mannerism.

3. Deliberately Inject the Mannerism into Your Conversations

Once a day, make a conscious effort to vocalize your mannerism. It's hard to do, but it brings it to mind.

74

4. Practice Injecting and Removing Your Mannerism as You Read the Newspaper Aloud

"The Dow Jones Industrial Average is up today."

"The uh Dow Jones uh Industrial uh Average . . ."

"The Dow Jones Industrial Average is up today."

"The uh Dow Jones uh . . ."

With practice, your mannerism will disappear from your everyday speech.

PAUSES

A pause should only be long enough to establish your emphasis, usually one to three seconds. Too much of a pause, or too much pausing in a talk, is low impact. There is no right or wrong place for pauses, so long as they are brief and regular.

It doesn't matter where you take your pauses, but *take them so you mean them.*

SPEED

There is no correct speaking speed, but if you're beyond 160 words per minute, you're too fast. If you crawl at 110 words a minute, you're too slow.

People in control are never in a hurry. They generally

75

go a degree below normal and appear to use words carefully. They don't shift gears. Jerkiness of any kind signals lack of control. Practice as you do with pitch. Slow down and watch as the audience anticipates, speed up and they'll get a message of urgency. Avoid extremes either way. Enunciate clearly. Don't run words together as you try to get your point across.

INSTANT REVIEW

POWERVOICING

Your voice is probably your least utilized source of presentation power. There are many areas that can be improved with a little practice.

Inflection:
1. Upward inflection is when your voice rises slightly, as when you're asking a question.
2. Downward inflection occurs when volume and emphasis hammer in on a word or phrase.
3. Upward inflection is tentative; downward inflection is authoritative.
4. Practice your upward and downward inflection by reading from newspapers and magazines, underlining various words for emphasis.

Pitch:
1. Lower your voice by opening your mouth wider.
2. Loosen up with deep breathing.
3. Reach way down for a prolonged vowel sound.
4. Alternate with the less shallow vowel sound of your conversational speaking voice.

Volume:
1. Powervoicing is not being loud. Often, it's being softer.
2. Too loud is insecure.
3. Practice projecting your voice to the far corner of the room.
4. Watch the pros and how they use volume.

Breath control:
1. Keep diaphragmatic speech as your goal.
2. Develop strong posture.
3. Practice tapping the power of the diaphragm.

Mannerisms:
1. Mannerisms are harder to identify than to get rid of.
2. Write mannerism on a single index card and refer to it.
3. Put mannerism into your conversation deliberately.
4. Read the paper aloud, injecting mannerisms.
5. Alternate mannerism and mannerism-free speech for practice.

Rhythm:
1. You can influence your effect by deliberately emphasizing words or syllables.
2. Use pauses carefully and only to separate groups of words; keep them short. Take dramatic pauses deliberately.
3. The speech rhythm of a person in control is always deliberate.

Speed:
1. There's no right or wrong speed.
2. Monitor yourself and decide where you are.
3. Avoid extremes.
4. Enunciate clearly, don't run words together.

Punching up your voice:
1. Practice reading aloud and underlining words for volume.
2. Underline groups of words for pauses and emphasis.
3. Use slashes to separate phrases and indicate a pause.
4. Eventually, you'll underscore your main points automatically.

12

THE
Q&A SESSION

A QUESTION and answer session will follow virtually every presentation you give. Be cool, concise, and follow these steps:

1. Keep Your Energy Up

Don't relax when the formal presentation is over. Be ready to answer sharp questions.

2. "I Don't Know" Is a Valid Answer

If the question falls within the parameters of a well-prepared talk and you're not equipped to provide an answer, so what? Tell them you don't know.

3. Follow "I Don't Know" with Action and a Timetable

While not knowing the answer immediately is valid, leaving it that way is never enough:

Say: "I wouldn't hazard a guess on something so important, but if you leave me your card, I'll get you the answer by the end of the week."

Or, you can say: "Give me a few days after I return to Detroit. I'll call you Monday with the answer."

Of course, if it's an area only tangentially related to your field, you owe the questioner nothing. Still, it is higher impact to make, and keep, a promise: "That area isn't even remotely related to what I do, but a friend of mine knows the field well. If you leave me your card, I'll ask her to call you."

4. Watch for Two or Three Questions Posing as One

This is one of the all-time, world-class Q&A blunders. You hear two or three questions and you try to answer them in a few sentences.

Say: "I'm hearing two questions here. The first is about toxic waste. The second is about regulation. I can address the waste."

80

5. No Debates

There's always some clown who misses college bull sessions and wants to start one at your presentation. Answer the question and allow a follow-up to be courteous.

But then say: "I think this is getting too involved. I'd be delighted to discuss it with you in a few minutes when we're through."

The debater may come to you afterward, but without the audience, he or she won't be that interested.

6. Listen for Text and Subtext

Pay attention to notes of sarcasm, levity, or other emotions lurking between the words of the question. If the intent is to embarrass or draw attention away from you, be polite and brisk.

7. Repeat the Question When You Hear It

Obviously, a meeting of six people won't warrant repeating the question, but doing so usually helps people in the back of a room become better involved with what's going on. Repeating the question also clarifies the issue.

8. If You're in Doubt, Ask If Your Answer Is Satisfactory

As in: "Have I answered your question, Mr. Partridge?"

9. Never Dismiss the Questioner

Assume that there's no such thing as a stupid question or questioner. Privately, you may have your own feelings, but keep

81

them a secret. If these people are interested enough to ask, be flattered and provide a direct answer.

10. Answer Briefly

No tangents or war stories during the Q&A please. If it can't be answered in a minute or two, tell the person to see you after the session.

INSTANT REVIEW

THE Q&A SESSION

1. Keep your energy up—Q&A is still public speaking.
2. "I don't know" is a valid answer.
3. Follow "I don't know" with action and a timetable.
4. Watch for two or three questions posing as one.
5. No debates.
6. Listen for text and subtext.
7. Repeat the question when you hear it.
8. If you're in doubt, ask the questioner if you've answered the question.
9. Never dismiss the questioner.
10. Keep answers brief.

13

WORKING
WITH VISUALS

S L I D E S, videos, filmstrips, computer graphics, transparencies, flip charts, and other audiovisual devices are a constant in corporate life. While it is not our intent to familiarize you with the idiosyncrasies of modern audiovisual systems, knowing a few basics will help you make better decisions with them.

FIVE REASONS TO USE VISUALS

1. They Divert Attention from You

Visuals fill out the stage or meeting room. There's more to watch than a single talking head.

2. They Reduce Stagefright

Visuals take away the sense of being alone and divert some of the awesome responsibility of keeping an audience's attention.

3. Visuals Clarify Data

Three-dimensional computer graphics can make any set of facts look thoughtful and intelligent. The audience appreciates the sensory diversion of visuals in presentations when there's a lot of data to absorb.

4. Visuals Often Increase Interest in the Topic

That's what the sales rep will tell you, anyway. So long as they aren't overused, visuals supplement a good presentation and raise the audience interest level by picking up the pace.

5. Visuals Increase Rentention

They may well forget your face or what you wore, but the audience will usually remember a good visual.

THREE REASONS NEVER TO USE VISUALS

1. Because You Have Stagefright

Visuals *help* with stagefright, but they're not a pill. For the nonphobic (which includes most of us despite overuse of the term), the only cure is grueling, galley slave rehearsal. Bells and whistles will only go so far; if you have severe fright, they may well make it worse.

2. To Fill Time

There's no such thing as a well-prepared talk that runs too short. If you cover your topic before the allotted time, there's too much allotted time. Finish up and leave the stage.

3. Because It Looks Like Fun and You Like to Experiment

Visuals, especially video, can make you feel like you're directing movies. However, you can produce your way to boredom, not to mention the horror of trying to compensate when they don't work.

TEN TIPS FOR USING VISUALS EFFECTIVELY

1. You Are the Best Visual in the Room

The way you walk, dress, hold the room, and zero in for a one-to-one talk with your audience should be paramount in your planning. Use visuals sparingly to augment your natural leadership.

85

2. Think Small Before Large

A ball bearing that killed a family of four or a defective beverage bottle that resulted in a $3 million settlement might be far more effective than a slide presentation, film, or video.

3. Place Visuals in Your Presentation to Accentuate Your Central Theme, Not the Other Way Around

Many speakers fall in love with a visual only peripherally related to their main thesis, then try to stretch. What they really stretch is their credibility.

4. Keep Everything Large

Use uppercase lettering, large numbers, projection video monitors if available, and elevated screens for films, slides, and transparencies. Lines and drawings on charts should be bold and heavy.

5. Avoid

Too much detail in a visual aid

Blackboards (they don't reflect light well and everyone hates them anyway)

Crowding of lettering

6. Test Everything Ahead of Time

That includes plugs that you've been assured work, flip charts, transparencies, the angles of elevated visuals, and all equipment.

86

When something goes wrong later, the only help you'll get from the hotel or conference center staff is momentum-killing delay and lame excuses about it working yesterday.

7. Keep Visuals Out of Your Way, and Invisible to the Audience, Until You Need Them

If they're obtrusive, visuals will impair your delivery. Keep them, if not out of sight altogether, then to one side, below the lectern, or otherwise away from center stage.

8. Talk to the Audience, Not to the Visual

There is a strong temptation when working with a screen visual to shift toward it as you speak. Continue to address your audience once you've assured yourself that the apparatus is in place and functioning.

9. Don't Stand in Front of the Visual

10. Don't Allow the Visual to Block Your Audience's View of You

WORKING WITH VISUALS

Five reasons to use visuals:
1. They divert attention from you.
2. They reduce stagefright.
3. They clarify data.
4. They increase interest in the topic.
5. They increase retention.

Three reasons never to use visuals:
1. Don't use them to relieve your stagefright.
2. Don't use them to fill time.
3. Don't use them because they look like fun.

Ten tips for using visuals effectively:
1. You are your own best visual.
2. Think small before large.
3. Use visuals to accentuate your central idea, not the other way around.
4. Keep everything large.
5. Avoid too much detail.
6. Test everything ahead of time.
7. Keep visuals out of your way until you need them.
8. Talk to the audience, not the visual.
9. Don't stand in front of the visual.
10. Don't allow the visual to block the audience's view of you.

14

TIPS
FOR
PRESENTING
AT MEETINGS

HIGH PRIORITY MEETINGS are as charged as anything you'll do from a stage. All the high impact preparation and delivery strategies apply. Here are six additional tips:

1. Let Them See and Hear You

The Politburo seems laid back compared to the seating structure at corporate meetings. The acoustics aren't wonderful, and you might have to do your piece from your chair. If possible, stand up. If the seating arrangement dictates against it, sit up straight so you can use your diaphragm to its maximum and project your voice to the farthest wall.

2. You Can't Always Play to Everyone

The geometry of conference seating arrangements—rectangles, circles, herringbones—might dictate improvised eye contact. If the arrangement is awkward, such as having people behind you, take the time to move to the best vantage point you can find and, as usual, use all of your upper body to play to them. If there are still people you can't reach, that's life. Don't dilute your force by turning yourself into a pretzel to accommodate an impossible situation.

3. The Agenda Goes Off Course

If you're not running the meeting, you might not even finish your presentation. Prepare to lobby for your own position on center stage and to assert your need to complete your talk. It may be up to you to diplomatically push the agenda back on course.

4. A Good Chunk of Your Audience Might Not Want to Be There

The audience in a meeting is often a reluctant one. While they're listening to you, their assistants are probably trying to put out the little brushfires that always start when they're out of reach. Write a percentage of them off as you prepare.

90

5. Meeting Speaking Is More Concrete

Tell them when you plan to do something, when the first step will be completed, how you plan to report the progress, how much it will cost, and the personnel involved.

6. Brevity Is a Power Tool

The boss might have a limo, a company jet, and three residences, but he does not, and never will, have enough time. Being poised and concise will earn you more points than joining the pack of whiners, carpers, loudmouths, and bullies who just have to fill the ether with their presence.

INSTANT REVIEW

PRESENTING AT MEETINGS

1. Let them see and hear you.
2. Get the best position you can for eye contact.
3. The agenda may go off course—be prepared.
4. A piece of your audience might not want to be there.
5. Meeting speaking is more concrete.
6. Brevity is a power tool.

THE ROOM

Entertainers talk about "the room" with the clear-eyed professionalism of an athlete sizing up a stadium or court:

"Nice town, crummy room.
I wouldn't play there again."

"The room's quiet tonight."

"Great room!"

Every nightclub owner and television producer has a horror story about a featured performer saying, "I can't do my act in this room," and walking out. Such performance-oriented reverence seems to be lost on the architects, conference planners, and audiovisual people responsible for the dungeons where we give our most critical presentations. The acoustics are often lousy, the mikes don't work, the lighting produces migraines, and the carpeting smells like it's been sprayed with something dangerous.

Control is often a function of setting. Here are tips for speaking in five of the most typical business settings.

1. The Conference Room

Eye contact is everything in the conference room. Notes are okay, but only in the most peripheral way. A conference room presentation has to look extemporaneous. Stand where the decision-makers can see you.

If company protocol allows it, standing is much better than

sitting. Stand in the middle or on either end, and do not walk around. You're not teaching seventh grade here.

The acoustics usually aren't so hot, so you might need more volume than you think.

2. The Theatrical Layout

This is the basic auditorium setting with you on stage, or at the bottom of a hill of rows. There is a wall between your audience and you in this setting; it's not a great environment for pacing or inviting a lot of audience participation.

The theatrical setup is for information—you to them, not the other way around. The visibility is good enough for slides, videos, flip charts, and other visuals.

Amplification is often a must. If the audiovisual department hasn't miked the place, you may have to force the issue. Few things are worse than choruses of "Can't hear you " when amplification has not been anticipated.

3. Team Seating

When the audience is broken into small circular discussion groups for problem solving, get to the high ground, and get a mike—preferably one of those wireless jobs so you can later walk around and capitalize on the participatory spirit of the teams. For the informational part of your talk, you should be on a raised platform, stage, or some other place where the audience can see you. Expect cross talk. Once you seat people in small groups facing one another, you have created a zoo. Team seating is not for the simple dissemination of information. It is the arrangement of choice for long problem-solving sessions.

93

4. Classroom Seating

You never get away from this numbing seating arrangement. Every time the company sends you off to yet another Marriott or Holiday Inn for training, you go through a couple of days seated at tables separated by aisles.

If you're conducting a seminar, training session, or some other lecture-oriented presentation, the classroom arrangement is ideal.

Most hotels are now very good at accommodating visuals, but check it out ahead of time.

If you are a pacer, arrange the seats in a herringbone pattern, so people can keep track of you. Amplification is a little short in these settings. The hotel might furnish a miked lectern, but you'll only use it if your presentation keeps you in front of the class all day. If you have to walk from table to table for more hands-on instruction, you'll have to speak up.

5. The Senate Seating Arrangement

Each row has its own elevated level, like the U.S. Senate. The acoustics are very good in such rooms, and designed for modern audiovisual equipment, especially videotape. Eye contact suffers because your audience is elevated and you're looking up at them. Give this arrangement a fair shot. After a little discomfort, it becomes easy to work.

94

INSTANT REVIEW

THE ROOM

1. The conference room: Stand, if possible; don't let the corporate structure prevent your taking a position where people can see you. Play to the decision-makers by standing opposite them. Eye contact is paramount.
2. Theatrical seating: Perfect for informational speeches involving minimal audience participation. Not good for give-and-take situations. Information passes from speaker to audience.
3. Team seating: Get where they can see you, use a mike, and expect cross talk. Team seating is participatory by nature.
4. Classroom seating: Good for seminars, training, and other instructional communication. Set in a herringbone pattern if you like to walk and talk at the same time.
5. Senate seating: Acoustically good and adaptable for any speaking goal.

IMPROMPTU SPEAKING

"I believe Jennifer has a few thoughts on that. She's been working on the project for some time."

"Bob was in St. Louis last week. Bob, can you come up here and just give us your take on their operation?"

We don't always pick our speaking opportunities. Sometimes we're on the spot to get up there and do the job right. An impromptu talk is a talk, with all the strategies of any corporate speaking situation. Your voice needs to be tuned, your body language put in place, eye contact working to your advantage, and you have to be as authoritative as ever.

Here are five tips that will help when you're put on the spot.

1. Impromptu Speaking Is Not Accidental

The brief, nonscheduled speaking setting usually reflects the management style of a single key individual. Good leaders move around and radiate their energy; they don't know how to live behind a desk.

Develop a *strategy* for extemporaneous speaking situations. Learn to recognize them long before you're called.

2. Keep Critical Information Nearby

If you think you might be called to the front of the room, write key facts on an index card and keep it in your pocket or purse. Now you have a safety net.

3. Take Your Time

Remember your stagecraft. When you're put on the spot, there's a temptation to hurry. This blows your control. Take a second to walk to the front of the room, to remove your notes, put on your reading glasses, and face your audience. This brief action guards against stammering, quivers in your voice, and other mannerisms. It gives you the control you need.

4. Speak to One Person

The conversational tone is hard to find when someone asks you to leave your seat and speak. Find or visualize one friendly face and talk as though you're having a conversation with that person. It's an old speech trick that works especially well here.

5. Be Especially Brief

You'll be impressive if you snap to the occasion, produce the information right away, and rattle everything off in the most authoritative tone you can find. Once you've earned those points, get off fast. You'll probably dilute your effect if you stay up too long.

97

INSTANT REVIEW

IMPROMPTU SPEAKING

1. Impromptu speaking is not an accident; develop a strategy for it.
2. Keep critical information nearby.
3. Take your time.
4. Speak to a single person.
5. Be especially brief.

15

DEFENDING AGAINST CRITICISM WITHOUT APPEARING DEFENSIVE

SOMEONE is always out to put you on the defensive. It can be strategy, management style, a way of communicating, a ploy to impress senior people at the meeting, or an honest, if misguided, method of getting information by playing the devil's advocate. But regardless of what it is, it's never pleasant.

This chapter will provide you with several strategies for holding your ground when you are criticized. It often stings, but it's part of the game we play.

1. Criticism Is Not Your Enemy

There's a child in all of us waiting to either hide and cry or strike back when we hear criticism of our ideas. All of our education and polish never seem to be enough to counter this tendency to confuse criticism with personal attack.

Yet we learn from criticism. Many of our most productive actions come from a recognition of areas in our lives that need improvement. We look back fondly at events that revolutionized our thinking, perhaps even made our careers, and find they usually started with someone's constructive advice. Criticism of any kind is never fun, but it loses its bite as time separates us from the circumstances that bring it about. Resign yourself to criticism. Think of the poor unproductive fool who has nothing in his or her life to criticize.

2. Arguments in Business Are Not Tennis Matches

Only one person wins a tennis match. That makes the opponent a loser. Such a simple approach to business arguments is not possible, and if you view each objection to your ideas or actions as a serve, you probably need to reevaluate your career goals.

3. The Way You React to Criticism Will Be More Vividly Remembered Than the Argument You Present

That statement reflects the same principle that applies to any form of delivery, whether you're appearing before a large audience, a television camera, or in a small meeting. How you respond to objection will be a permanent part of your corporate image.

100

4. Don't Raise Your Voice

There are plenty of opportunities to use the full force of volume, but dealing with criticism is not one of them. Go home and punch the wall if you must, but, in the office, stay cool when they don't like your ideas.

5. Listen Attentively to the Criticism

Listening is often blocked by emotion. Carefully weigh the words as you hear them and, if possible, avoid the temptation to poison your thinking with defensive counterarguments. Take a beat and just listen.

6. Move Forward

Even if some clown is throwing a tantrum and pointing his index finger at your face, lean forward and remain calm. Physically invade your attacker's space a hair while showing no emotion.

7. Never Use Inflammatory Language

If you call someone a jerk and say he wouldn't know a good idea if it ran over his thick head, you have taken that person out of your life for a few years. Your shot at cooperation for this, and future, conflicts is somewhere between zero and minus five.

Most of us are smart enough to avoid profanity or overtly hostile words. Few of us ever learn to stop using dismissive or conde-scending language.

101

8. Look for Areas of Agreement

It may be hard to believe, but you and the person criticizing your work may be after the same goals. See if you can locate your area of commonality and use it as a reference point.

9. Stick to Issues and Evidence

The winner always uses the language of reason. Invoke the good of the company, your common goals, or the logic of your position. Keep the evidence unemotional.

10. Store Key Points of Their Argument for Future Use

You may not walk away from a particular confrontation with the upper hand, but you may fortify a future position by taking careful note of your meeting partner's criticism.

11. Clarify as You Go Along

As in: "Let me see if I'm clear here, Joe. You never seek commissions, but you feel you're entitled to one on this deal. You are also aware that our company never pays commissions under these circumstances."

12. Be Open to the Criticism

Even if you'd like to boil this twerp in his own body fluids, remain open and conciliatory in tone. Here are several techniques for achieving this effect:

102

Negative Assertion: You agree with the criticism, sometimes because you've even seen the light. More often, negative assertion is used to take the momentum from an attacker.

A Conciliatory Statement: A conciliatory statement comes when you realize you've been a jerk and don't want to say so. Or you've reached a point where you've got to give something in order to make further gains in the negotiation: "I think I might have overreacted, but you can understand where I was coming from. I'm open to further discussion before I make up my mind."

A Statement of Self-disclosure: A statement of self-disclosure expresses your feelings immediately: "I'm *very angry* about not seeing those forms before they went out." Or, "I am *confident* that we can put this problem behind us and get down to the business of selling our new line."

Fogging: Fogging acknowledges the criticism while indicating an unwillingness to dwell on it. For example: "There may be some truth to what you say." Or, "That's a thought." And, "I see what you mean."

13. Don't Argue with Petty People

You'll find people willing to go to war over whether junior executives should be given their own stationery. Paper clips and their distribution can be a life-or-death issue for some people. When you encounter this kind of assault, one that you feel has no validity, diplomatically acknowledge the complaint and tell the person you don't feel it is germane to the topic of today's meeting. Petty people usually aren't going much further. Don't get sucked in by them.

103

INSTANT REVIEW

DEFENDING AGAINST CRITICISM

1. Criticism is not your enemy.
2. Arguments are not tennis matches.
3. The way you react to criticism will be more vividly remembered than the argument you present.
4. Don't raise your voice.
5. Listen attentively to the criticism.
6. Move forward (physically).
7. Never use inflammatory language.
8. Look for areas of agreement.
9. Stick to issues and evidence.
10. Store key points of their argument for future use.
11. Clarify as you go along.
12. Be open to your criticism.
   With negative assertion
   With a conciliatory statement
   With a statement of self-disclosure
   By fogging
13. Don't argue with petty people.

16

HEAD TO HEAD: EFFECTIVE PRESENTATIONS TO A SINGLE INDIVIDUAL

MANY of our most important "speeches" are presentations to a single individual—be it a boss, a potential employer, or a colleague who can save a lot of steps. While we are willing to plunge into weeks of preparation for a platform speech or seminar, these one-to-one sessions often get shortchanged.

The following tips, when combined with other high impact techniques, will help strengthen your skills in one-to-one communication.

1. Get to the Meeting Unencumbered

Leave your raincoat, umbrella, overcoat, packages, and other distractions in the reception area.

2. When You Visit Someone in His or Her Office, Make That Person Come to You

Don't dash across the room to kiss a ring. Move directly toward your host, but let him meet you halfway.

3. Be a Respectful Equal

Even when your host has a lot of clout, don't let your body language fawn. Be professional, show the proper respect for rank, but stand tall and show that you're in charge of your own life.

4. Don't Enter Talking or Talk Too Much

If you come into the room talking, or start filling conversational voids compulsively, you send a signal of nervousness and uncertainty.

5. Clear Your Hands Before the Handshake

If you're carrying a briefcase or charts, move them to your left hand or set them on the chair where you expect to sit; then shake hands.

106

6. Get Right to the Point

A few social amenities, then go right for it. Directness commands respect.

7. Turn Your Body Squarely Toward Your Partner

As with a platform speech, turn your whole body toward your audience. You send a message of confidence and conviction.

8. Check for Understanding as You Go Along

Make sure you're getting your idea across. As you go through your presentation, break it up with short inquiries: "To summarize where we are, June, you want to see a better degree of cooperation between our departments, you find my assistant arrogant to yours, and you're unhappy about the timetable. Is that what I'm hearing, so far?"

9. Present with a Concise Plan

Your intro, main body, and conclusion are less formal, perhaps, but you should know precisely which points should be covered before you begin your talk. Build toward a finish.

10. Place Yourself in Your Partner's Position

As you would with a room full of conventioneers, ask yourself what you would want if the positions were reversed.

107

INSTANT REVIEW

EFFECTIVE PRESENTATIONS
TO A SINGLE INDIVIDUAL

1. Get there unencumbered.
2. Make the person cross the room, or meet you halfway.
3. Be a respectful equal.
4. Don't enter talking or talk too much.
5. Clear your hands before the handshake.
6. Get right to the point.
7. Turn your whole body squarely toward your partner.
8. Check for understanding as you go along.
9. Present with a concise plan.
10. Place yourself in your partner's position.

17

THE
BUSINESS
LUNCH

BUSINESS LUNCHES are here to stay. Tax laws may yank away some of the loopholes for a more clear distinction between business and recreation, but American business moves over food. The following twelve tips will help you prepare your luncheon presentations.

1. Walk into the Restaurant with an Agenda, However Informal

A lunch meeting needs direction. Don't randomly waltz in and out of topics just because you're in a less formal setting.

2. Jot

Don't whip out the legal-size pad as soon as you're seated, but when business gets under way, and you know your partner is making important points, jot them down. Otherwise, you could get back to the office and leave out an important follow-up step.

3. Avoid Watering Holes

Industry hangouts are great for career advancement, but you wouldn't conduct important, confidential meetings where your competitor might be a table away. As you probably well know, watering holes are staffed by gossipy people who have been known to earn better tips by reporting what they hear.

4. Don't Lunch When You're Angry at the Person You're Meeting

Angry meetings are for closed doors. Controlled tempers can get out of control, and you could easily find yourself the butt of insider gossip and jokes after a spectacle.

5. Watch the Booze

The so-called three-martini lunch is largely an anachronism of the 1950s, but it's not totally gone. Many executives with clout (who may have been doing this back in the fifties) will down a couple before even thinking about business. If you're not up to the capacity of your partner, don't be a sport. You won't know what hit you.

And if you're not quite a part of today's Perrier lunch crowd, don't feel you have a license to get a buzz on just because you and your buddies have been doing things this way for years.

6. Watch the Smoke

If you smoke and your partner doesn't, you're probably going to lose out by smoking at the meal. Even if he or she professes not to mind, a nonsmoker always minds. And you know how former smokers go on about how bad cigarettes smell and taste.

7. Work Toward a Single Objective

Can you make the deal in one meal? If not, your objective should be to fortify the relationship with a follow-up action. Or you may think you can bag the whole thing by coffee. Regardless of your objective, always have a specific place you want to be by the time the check is paid.

8. Build Follow-Up into the Lunch

As with any meeting, leave with homework on your or your partner's part, something to continue the dialogue even if things haven't gone especially well.

111

9. Use a Low Key Presentation Style

Nice and easy does it at lunch. Plant your feet in cement as you would on stage, sit up straight, look directly at your partner, and pitch with a distinct sense of where you're going, as you would in a formal talk. At lunch, the voice only has to go across a table, so you want a nice low pitch. A luncheon presentation is poised and free of pyrotechnics.

10. Build Toward Your Conclusion as You Would with Any Other Speech

Don't appear to be in a hurry. Between the appetizer and coffee, you will be in the company of your dining partner or partners for at least an hour. Maybe you know these people socially and you want to get the business out of the way so you can discuss other things. Fine, just don't rush your presentation. Build to something.

11. Expect to Be Interrupted

Your partner will want you to clarify as you go along and will probably ask questions. Be receptive, and diplomatically get back on the track.

INSTANT REVIEW

THE BUSINESS LUNCH

1. Don't lunch if you can get the job done somewhere else.
2. Have an agenda.
3. Jot things down.
4. Avoid watering holes.
5. Don't lunch when you're angry.
6. Watch the booze.
7. Watch the smoke.
8. Work toward a single objective.
9. Build follow-up into the lunch.
10. Use a low-key presentation style.
11. Build toward a conclusion.
12. Expect to be interrupted.

18

COCKTAILS AT SEVEN, DINNER AT EIGHT: TIPS FOR PRESENTING YOUR IDEAS AT SOCIAL OCCASIONS

N HER BOOK *Letitia Baldridge's Guide to Executive Manners*, former Kennedy administration protocol chief Letitia Baldridge gives a vivid example of the number one rule for business social occasions: it's better to ask than wing it.

An executive was hosting a fancy dinner for his company's clients. When the sommelier asked him to choose a wine, he did so with authority. So far, so good. But when the steward returned with the host's choice, the man found himself in a very bad spot. The steward presented him with the cork and he didn't know what to do with it. Everyone at the table began to look into his or her lap as the poor guy stared, baffled, at the cork, hoping maybe it would tell him what happens next. He must have figured the show goes on, so improvise. He bit off the tip of the cork, swirled it around, again with great authority, and swallowed it. Then he nodded his approval.

Don't be so sure you wouldn't do something equally off the wall. Most of us wouldn't eat a cork, but we might try to tip the help at an exclusive club, or say something inadvertently offensive. If you look, and are truthful, there is some version of that cork back there in your corporate life.

If you've never picked up Ms. Baldridge's fine book, or any of the dozen or so volumes on corporate protocol, do so. We don't know what we don't know.

All the rules of a talk apply to a cocktail party or executive dinner—powervoicing, body language, eye contact, and a careful presentation. The conference room and platform speech techniques will serve you well.

Walk in confidently. Entering a business/social occasion is walking onstage, and your posture, body language, and general countenance should be the best it can be. Have you given the event enough priority, and yourself enough time to freshen up? Here are some tips that apply to cocktail parties and business dinners.

1. Introduce a Junior Person to a Senior Person, and a Younger Person to an Older Person

The junior person is presented *to* the senior person, the unofficial person *to* the official individual. As in: "Congresswoman Stenhouse, I'd like you to meet our executive vice president, Jerry Moss." Or, "Mr. Moss, this is my assistant, Tom Morrison."

2. Know When to Use, and Not Use, First Names

Back in the office, your boss might be just Jerry. When there are civilians around, however, he might want to be called Mr. Moss.

You are probably on a first-name basis with your secretary, especially when you are going through a time of high stress. But when the boss is around, or your peers, you would probably get annoyed at the liberty of being addressed too casually by one of your staff.

3. Don't Discuss Business in Mixed Company

Many executives have very strong feelings about discussing business when their families are present. Even when everyone at the occasion is working toward a common corporate goal, you can make an enormous blunder by bringing up some office crisis.

4. Don't Interrupt

5. Be Attentive

Don't be anticipating your next point as your conversation partner makes hers. Pay attention and comment thoughtfully. In a

117

social setting, you have an opportunity of access and informal conversation that you do not have in an office. Maximize that opportunity by being a good listener.

REMEMBERING NAMES

Memory experts construct keys for associating names with faces. There are courses and books on this topic. One problem is that the skill is similar to speed reading. When you come out of the course, or put down the book, you're impressive enough to appear on the "Tonight Show." If you don't practice, the skill fades. Still, it's a great, and imperative, ability in business. Here are a few things to remember.

1. Take a Second to Repeat the Name When You Are Introduced

Find an excuse to repeat the name aloud if need be: "Nice to meet you, Jerry. I'm sorry, I missed your last name."
Get it right there and you'll retain it better.

2. Form a Mental Image Based on the Name

Suppose Jerry says his last name is Tatum. Tatum sounds like a "tater" or potato. Think of Jerry as a potato, and Tatum should come back. Any silly association will do.

3. Write Down Every Name You Can Remember After the Party

If you don't do this, the only thing you'll remember about Jerry is potato. Jerry Potato. Nice work. But if you get home and write down Jerry Tatum and a little summary of ole Jer, you'll have him next time.

4. Form a Mental Picture Linking the Person with the Conversation

Jerry Tatum mentioned his passion for sailing. Now you have a potato in a sailboat. You have fortified the image even further. The next time you meet Jerry, you will remind him that the two of you talked about sailing. It will be your secret that you remembered this wonderful thing by picturing a potato rigging a sail.

5. Link the Picture with the Location Where You First Saw the Person

Jerry Potato is now sailing through the Hyatt Regency ballroom with a cocktail in his hand.

There is no one right way to use word and face association; there are many techniques that should work for you. Your system has to make sense to no one but yourself. Let's face it. Anything is better than just trying to repeat names. The process of linking images is cumbersome only at first. Within a week or so, you'll do it subconsciously, and you'll be very impressive.

When you remember someone's name and a little

about his or her identity, you score points immediately. It's worth the effort.

INSTANT REVIEW

PRESENTING YOUR IDEAS AT SOCIAL OCCASIONS

1. Introduce a junior person to a senior person, and a younger person to an older person.
2. Know when first names are, and are not, appropriate.
3. Don't discuss business in mixed company.
4. Don't interrupt.
5. Be attentive.

To remember names:

1. Take a second to repeat a name when you are introduced.
2. Form a mental image based on the name.
3. Write down names when you get home or back to the office.
4. Form a mental picture linking the person with your conversation.
5. Link the image with the location where you first saw the person.

19

THE ELOQUENCE OF THE GOOD LISTENER

WE LEAVE YOU with advice to be a better listener. It is such a powerful tool that you could run an ad in the back of an adventure magazine promising: "Secret word revealed for money and power beyond imagination. Send $14.95 and live well forever."

Study after study shows that miscommunication occurs largely because we don't know how to listen. Choose the five biggest business hassles you've had in the past year, and think about what went wrong:

"Oh, you mean shipping? *Why didn't you say* shipping? *I thought you meant receiving."*

"You never said that. What you said was . . ."

"I could swear you said, 'Buy a truck,' so I bought a truck. If you didn't say, 'Buy a truck,' what did you say?"
"I said don't buy a truck."

Here are six tips for good listening.

1. Look Directly at the Speaker

2. Concentrate Hard on His Words Instead of Where He's Going Next

3. Interrupt When He's Losing You

It's not impolite to slow a person down if he's galloping ahead of you. Ask for clarification of the point.

4. Recap

Sum up the main points as you go along, either directly to the speaker or to yourself.

5. Look for the Interesting Points

Chances are that anyone you're speaking with is saying something of direct interest to you. You might have to look for it, but it will be there.

122

6. Don't Finish His Thoughts

Some people take forever to make a point. We know where they're going, so we "help out" by completing the thought for them. In doing so, we can create fluster and an unintentional memory of rudeness.

INSTANT REVIEW

THE ELOQUENCE OF THE GOOD LISTENER

1. Look directly at the speaker.
2. Concentrate on his words instead of where he's going next.
3. Interrupt when the speaker is losing you.
4. Recap as you go along.
5. Focus on finding interesting aspects of the subject matter.
6. Don't complete the speaker's thoughts.

FOR
FURTHER
READING

Avery, Elizabeth; Dorsey, Jane; Sickles, Vera; *First Principles of Speech Training*. New York: Appleton-Century Crofts, 1928.

Bachner, Jane, and Janet Stone, *Speaking Up: A Book for Every Woman Who Wants to Speak Effectively*. New York: McGraw-Hill, 1977.

Baldridge, Letitia, *Letitia Baldridge's Guide to Executive Manners*. New York: Warner Audio Publishing, 1986.

Bienstock, Eric, *Creative Problem Solving*. New York: Warner Audio Publishing, 1985.

Blanchard, E.B., "Brief Flooding Treatment for a Debilitating Revulsion." *Behavior Therapy*, Vol. 4 (1973), p. 581.

125

Bramson, Robert, Ph.D., *Coping with Difficult People*. New York: Simon & Schuster Audio and Video Publishing Division, 1986.

Butkowski, Alan, *The Complete Memory System for Names and Faces*. Chicago: Nightingale-Conant Corporation, 1984.

Cox, Danny, *Leadership When the Heat's On*. Albuquerque: Newman Communications Corp., 1985.

Crocker, Lionel, and Herbert W. Hildebrandt, *Public Speaking for College Students*. New York: American Book Company, 1956.

Delmar, Ken, *Winning Moves: The Body Language of Selling*. Albuquerque: Newman Communications Corporation, 1985.

Detz, Joan, *How to Write and Give a Speech*. New York: St. Martin's Press, 1984.

Doyle, Michael, and David Straus, *How to Make Meetings Work*. New York: Jove, 1985.

Drucker, Peter, *Taking Charge*. New York: American Management Association, 1982.

Einstein, Charles, *Communicating with Results*. New York: Warner Audio Publishing, 1985.

Eisen, Jeffrey, Ph.D., with Pat Farley, *Powertalk*. New York: Simon & Schuster, 1984.

Emery, Gary, *A New Beginning: How You Can Change Your Life Through Cognitive Therapy*. New York: Simon & Schuster, 1981.

Esquire Success Series, *Persuasive Speaking: Making Effective Speeches and Presentations*. New York: Esquire-Serendipity Associates, 1985.

Fast, Julius, *Body Language*. New York: M. Evans & Co., 1969.

Fishman, Scott M., and David W. Sheehan, "Anxiety and Panic: Their Cause and Treatment." *Psychology Today*, Vol. 19, No. 4, April 1985.

Fleming, Carol, Ph.D., *The Sound of Your Voice*. Albuquerque: Newman Communications Corporation, 1986.

Frank, Milo O., *How to Get Your Point Across in 30 Seconds or Less*. New York: Simon & Schuster Audio and Video Publishing, 1985.

Freudenberger, Herbert J., and Gail North, *Situational Anxiety*. Garden City, NY: Anchor Press, 1982.

Friedman, Edward, *The Complete Speechmaker's Handbook*. New York: Harper & Row, 1955.

126

Funk, Peter, *Word Power*. New York: Warner Audio Publishing, 1984.

Funk, Wilfred, *Six Weeks to Words of Power*. New York: Pocket Books, 1953.

Funk, Wilfred, and Norman Lewis, *30 Days to a More Powerful Vocabulary*. New York: Pocket Books, 1942.

Goodwin, Donald W., *Phobia: The Facts*. London: Oxford University Press, 1983.

Henley, Nancy, *Body Politics*. Englewood Cliffs, NJ: Prentice-Hall, 1979.

Hull, Raymond, *Successful Public Speaking*. New York: Harper & Row, 1971.

Jeffries, James R., and Jefferson D. Bates, *The Executive's Guide to Meetings, Conferences, and Audiovisual Presentations*. New York: McGraw-Hill, 1983.

Kent, Fraser, *Nothing to Fear: Coping with Phobias*. Garden City, NY: Doubleday, 1971.

Korda, Michael, *Power!* New York: Random House, 1975.

Lang, Doe, *Charisma*. New York: Warner Audio Publishing, 1984.

McCormack, Mark H., *Succeeding and Rising to the Top of Any Corporation*, New York: Warner Audio Publishing, 1985.

Marks, I.M., *Fears and Phobias*. London: Heinemann, 1969.

Montgomery, Robert L., *Effective Speaking for Managers*. Mount Laurel, NJ: Learn, Inc., 1984.

Nierenberg, Gerard, *The Art of Successful Negotiating*. Greenwich, CT: Network for Learning Cassettes, 1984.

Nierenberg, Gerard, *How to Read a Person Like a Book*. New York: Warner Audio Publishing, 1985.

Nierenberg, Gerard, and Henry H. Calero, *Between the Words: Hidden Meanings in What People Say*. New York: Simon & Schuster Audio and Video Publishing, 1985.

Prochnow, Herbert V., *The Successful Speaker's Handbook*. Englewood Cliffs, NJ: Prentice-Hall, 1969.

Sarnoff, Dorothy, *Speech Can Change Your Life*. New York: Dell, 1972.

Snyder, Elayne, *The Persuasive Speaker*, New York: Warner Audio Publishing, 1984, 1985.

127

Snyder, Elayne, and Jane Field, *Speak for Yourself with Confidence.* New York: New American Library, 1983.

Soper, Paul L., *Basic Public Speaking.* New York: Oxford University Press, 1963.

Toastmasters International, *Be Prepared to Speak.* San Francisco: Kantola-Skeie Productions, 1985.

Waitley, Dennis E., *The Psychology of Winning.* Listen and Learn, 1983.

The Wall Street Journal, The Best of the Manager's Journal. Albuquerque: Newman Communications, 1986.

The Wall Street Journal, The Wall Street Journal on Management. New York: Warner Audio Publishing, 1986.